A ... t

EXETER

Geoff Williams

Bossiney Books · Launceston

First published 2008 by Bossiney Books Ltd,
Langore, Launceston, Cornwall PL15 8LD
www.bossineybooks,com

ISBN 978-1-906474-04-1

Acknowledgements
The cover photograph is by Robert Hesketh
The prints are from the publishers' own collection

Printed in Great Britain by R Booth Ltd, Mabe, Cornwall

Exeter in 1765. The city was still largely contained within its ancient walls

Introduction

Exeter has a long and fascinating history, over 2000 years of continuous settlement, stretching back to at least the Iron Age. It remains one of England's most rewarding cities to study and explore. Every major stage of the city's history can be traced on the ground and in its incomparable archives, whilst archaeology has revealed even more.

An excellent settlement site, seaport and crossroads, Exeter is ideally situated to be the region's economic and cultural capital. This has been so since its foundation. Today's street lines follow the patterns laid by Britons and Saxons and nearly three quarters of Exeter's city walls still stand, including long sections founded on durable Roman masonry.

Exeter also retains a wealth of historic buildings, despite a series of violent attacks and sieges, including sacking by Vikings and bombing by the equally vengeful Luftwaffe. The Cathedral with its two Norman towers and richly decorated west front is outstanding, as is the medieval Guildhall – the oldest municipal building still in regular use in England. Exeter's Quay, its ring of red stone churches and a range of timber framed houses (including one saved from development and moved on wheels to its present location) are sights no visitor should miss.

1 Early Exeter

Our ancestors chose settlement sites for good reasons. Exeter has a superb position, at a junction of ancient ridge roads. The chief of these roads was the Icknield Way, which ran across the length of Britain and entered Exeter on the line of High Street, terminating on the low cliff top overlooking the Exe.

Water transport was at least as important as road. Significantly, the Iron Age people knew Exeter as Isca, meaning 'water'. Isca stood at the lowest fording point on the Exe and the Dumnonii, who inhabited Cornwall, Devon and Somerset west of the Parrett, have left evidence of their occupation in the area of Bartholomew Street and Southernhay. As Isca was at the tidal limit of navigation by ships, they also had a trading post by the river bank. The site had natural advantages: here, next to a break in the low cliffs, the red sandstone formed a bench on which traders could congregate upriver of the marshes and mud.

Overseas trade prior to the Roman invasion is proved by finds of Hellenistic coins. The traders who visited Exeter in prehistoric times unloaded and loaded their vessels at the point where the dignified

Customs House (1680) now stands on Exeter Quay. Hides, cattle and leather are likely to have figured prominently in the cargoes.

Exeter had other points in its favour. The rich red soils of the surrounding countryside offered both corn and meat, whilst the river yielded abundant water, wildfowl and fish, including a superb run of salmon and sea trout. To find more water, Exonians had but to dig a few metres down into their gravelly soils. This was a particular advantage if the settlement were besieged, as it was to be many times, most recently in 1646 when Sir Thomas Fairfax captured Exeter for Parliament during the Civil War.

As a hilltop site protected by marsh and water to the west, Exeter was in an excellent defensive position. Being 16km upriver, it was both harder for seaborne raiders to discover and more difficult to surprise than a coastal settlement.

Nonetheless, the Romans established a full scale legionary fortress here, enclosing 15 hectares, around AD 50. It is uncertain how this happened. In AD 43 the Emperor Claudius invaded south-east England and established military control there. His general Vespasian then swept south-west through the territory of the Durotriges, centred on Dorset, taking many towns and fortresses. But whereas there is evidence of Vespasian's campaign further east, at Maiden Castle and South Cadbury for example, there is no evidence of conflict in Dumnonia other than a very unreliable medieval tradition.

Perhaps there were battles which have left no evidence, perhaps the Dumnonians had the sense to capitulate in time. But pre-Roman Britain was a patchwork of mini-states, often at war with each other, and some of them had treaties with Rome. It is quite possible that Dumnonia was a Roman ally and welcomed the Roman army. The base camp at Exeter gave the army good sea communications, and effectively encircled the Durotriges.

Archaeological excavations in 1990 revealed a smaller Roman fort occupying about 1.5 hectares overlooking Exeter Quay and the strategic fording place of Exe Bridges, with commanding views up and down the Exe. This Roman fort may pre-date the legionary fortress with its bath house on the adjoining hill, where the city centre now stands.

Like Exeter, Topsham is an excellent site and was settled early. It is perched on a tongue of land where the Clyst joins the Exe. The deep water channel of the Exe swings east and runs close to Topsham Quay. Appreciating these advantages, the Romans made what we know as Topsham an outport and perhaps a naval base for *Isca Dumnoniorum*

The Water Gate, taken down in 1815

(the Roman term for Exeter) about AD50, and linked them by road. Excavations have revealed that Topsham remained a small Romano-British town and port as late as AD400.

After the occupation, *Isca Dumnoniorum* continued to be the regional capital for the south-west peninsula – a position it has essentially maintained ever since. Around AD120-130, the city was radically re-developed, partly within the old legionary fortress, which was obsolete. A grid-iron street pattern, basilica, bath house, town hall and forum were built. The people who organised this were not expatriate Italians, but the romanised aristocrats and merchants of Dumnonia.

With customary Roman thoroughness, the enlarged settlement of 38 hectares was defended with an earth bank. This was upgraded around AD200 to a stone wall 4.5 metres high and 3 metres thick and its perimeter still defines central Exeter. The Guildhall, Cathedral and main shops all come within its compass and High Street crosses the centre of the walled city. Stretches of Roman masonry are still visible, mainly in the lower courses of the wall – the sections in West Street and Southernhay are particularly good, while sections of the bank can be seen in Rougemont Gardens and the Bishop's Palace Gardens. What we see is a wall repaired and upgraded many times, but the dressed purple stones of local volcanic ‘trap’ (an excellent hard building stone, widely used in the Exeter area) are distinctive and often Roman. They are mixed in with red Heavitree sandstone, used extensively from the fourteenth century, and later brick.

When the church of St Mary Major next to the Cathedral’s west front was demolished in the 1970s, the remains of the legionary bath house – the oldest cut stone and mortared building in Britain – were revealed and photographed. Extensive remains of the Anglo-Saxon Abbey were also revealed, before the site was protected with sand and grass. Further excavations were made around the Guildhall, Fore Street, Gandy Street and Catherine Street and showed abundant traces of orderly Roman wooden barrack blocks.

Roman rule always entailed road building. Nine Roman roads radiated from Exeter. One road took troops west to the fortlet at North Tawton. Another led east via Heavitree to Dorchester and beyond; one south to Topsham; one north-east to Bath and the Midlands. The south-western road led across the Exe and over Haldon to Teignbridge, where the foundations of a Roman bridge have been discovered within the structure of a bridge near Kingsteignton. This has led to speculation about a likely Roman bridge over the Exe near the present Exe Bridges.

Certainly the Romans were accomplished bridge builders, but they may have been content simply to ford the Exe: the river was then wider and thus generally shallower and fordable at low tide, though later evidence shows fording the Exe could be dangerous to man and beast.

Isca Dumnoniorum was an important trading and civic centre, as the many coins found testify. Its population in the fourth century was perhaps 3000. Some were evidently people of standing: one large Roman town house had three ranges of rooms and a courtyard. Two rooms had hypocausts (underfloor heating).

It is conventionally assumed that the Romans withdrew from Britain in AD410. In fact the Roman army probably left Britain in 407, but well before that economic decline had set in. Exeter’s suburbs were abandoned around 360 and the town centre buildings gradually fell into decay over the next century.

In 568, the Dumnonii manned the walls against Cealwin, King of Wessex and again in 632 against Penda, King of Mercia. However, King Cenwealh of Wessex defeated them at Pinhoe in 658 and again at Crediton in 661. It was probably King Cenwealh who in 670 founded an Abbey on or near the site of the present Bishop’s Palace. Shortly afterwards, Saint Boniface, later missionary to the still heathen Germans, was educated here under Abbot Wolfhard.

Meanwhile, the defeated remnant of the British population occupied the area around Bartholomew Street, until they were expelled by King Athelstan in 928, who may have regarded them as a potential fifth column when the Danes came raiding. This district was called Britayne in medieval times – it was and is known as the West Quarter.

Whilst retaining a modified version of the British name *Isca*, the Wessex rulers added the Old English word *cæster* (indicating a Roman *castrum* or fort) and thus *Exancæster* was recorded in 894. The *Excestre* of 1086 was smoothed to Exeter by 1547. To avoid confusion we will refer to it as Exeter from now on.

Marauding Danes put local defences to the test in 851, but the men of *Defenascir* (Devonshire) drove them off. In 876, a Danish army overwintered within Exeter's walls, but were then driven out by King Alfred's forces. Probably Exeter's defences were strengthened after this salutary lesson. The present street grid may also date from this time.

In 893 another Danish force, finding the walls too hard to breach, besieged Exeter but fled on King Alfred's approach. King Athelstan rebuilt the city walls in 928 (the year he expelled the British), but Danes again laid siege in 1001. Finding the walls impenetrable, they set about pillaging the villages around. Men from Devon and Somerset fought them at Pinhoe (now part of Exeter), but were finally defeated. Pinhoe was burnt.

England's King, Ethelred the Unready (meaning 'ill-advised', rather than 'unprepared') provoked a further Danish attack by marrying Emma of Normandy (a rival power) and giving Exeter as a wedding gift to his new Norman bride. Worse still, in 1002 Ethelred ordered the massacre of the many Danish settlers in his realm, including the Danish King Svein's sister.

Svein attacked Exeter, an attractive target with its mint, and laid siege to it. Emma's Norman bailiff, Hugh, treacherously enabled the enemy to break into the city. The siege had already cost many lives, but Svein ordered Exeter's survivors to be massacred, its houses burnt and its churches pulled down.

Canute succeeded his father, Svein, and married the widowed Emma. He became king of England in 1016 and later of Denmark and Norway too, atoning for Svein's atrocity in Exeter and rebuilding the abbey church. When Bishop Leofric transferred his see from Crediton in 1050, Exeter's abbey church became the Cathedral.

Leofric donated the *Exeter Book* to the Cathedral Library. The largest extant collection of Old English literature, it was the fruit of the English

Benedictine revival of the 10th century and contains such famous poems as *The Wanderer*, *The Seafarer* and *The Ruin*, as well as a fascinating collection of riddles and the epic *Beowulf*, the most magnificent Old English poem of all. The book remains in Exeter.

2 Medieval Exeter

In 1066, at the time of the Norman Conquest, rebuilt Exeter had about 460 houses and 2500 inhabitants. Although small by today's standards, Exeter was approaching the size it had been during the Roman Empire. It was the tenth biggest town in England, with wealthy merchants and overseas trade. Thus it was essential for King William to control it.

English resistance continued after William's famous victory at Hastings. Exeter was the centre of the Western Rebellion of 1068-69. The citizens held it in great force, strengthening the walls and towers and encouraging other towns to defy the Normans.

Much alarmed, King William hastened back from Normandy and demanded an oath of fealty from Exeter's chief citizens. They refused to swear allegiance and would not admit William within their walls, although they did offer to pay tribute of eighteen pounds to him as king, the sum stipulated by ancient custom.

William angrily marched westwards with a combined Anglo-Norman army. He was met by the city's governing body 6 km outside the city. They entreated peace and agreed to bow to his commands, offering hostages. However, when they returned to Exeter bolder spirits repudiated the agreement.

William advanced on the city and found the gates shut and the walls manned. To frighten the citizens, he had one unfortunate hostage blinded in front of them. This barbarity only received an obscene gesture from a defender, so William laid siege. His men attacked the walls and tried to undermine them. Exeter held out for eighteen days in mid-winter. Conditions were hard for attacker and defender alike. Although the citizens must have been running short of supplies, William knew that while his forces were engaged attacking the city, the rest of Devon and Cornwall was free to defy him.

A compromise was reached. A procession of citizens, including women and clergy, prostrated themselves before William. He pardoned them and posted guards to prevent his troops from plundering Exeter. However, the king was obliged to swear that he would neither punish the citizens nor increase their customary tribute. It seems probable that William was also obliged to let King Harold's mother, Gytha and his sister, who had both sheltered in the city, go free.

Exeter had surrendered on favourable terms. To ensure its future obedience, the Normans immediately began building Rougemont Castle on the highest ground within the city walls. William moved west to subdue the rest of Devon and Cornwall, ordering castles to be built at Totnes, Launceston, Barnstaple and Okehampton to overawe the natives.

Rougemont still impresses, even in its ruined state, especially the massive gate tower beside the present entrance. This is the best preserved early Norman gatehouse keep in England.

One can readily appreciate how Baldwin, Earl of Devon, held out for three months in 1136 when besieged in Rougemont by King Stephen. England was in turmoil as Stephen disputed the crown with Matilda, daughter of Henry I. Baldwin supported Matilda and occupied Rougemont. When the citizens appealed to Stephen, Baldwin burnt part of the city and locked himself and his forces into Rougemont, surrendering only when the wells ran dry. He negotiated peace with Stephen and he and his men were spared.

With its growing population, Exeter could no longer rely on wells alone to provide it with enough water. The underground passages were begun about 1200 to supply water to the city from a spring at Lion's Holt. Over the centuries, a number of improvements were made to keep up with increased demand for water.

Meanwhile, Exeter had developed rapidly. 'By reason of its stateliness, the wealth of its citizens and the great resort of strangers, it so abounds with all sorts of merchandise, that nothing is wanting that can be reckoned useful,' according to William of Malmesbury in 1154.

This stateliness and wealth was also expressed in magnificent buildings, some of which still stand. Several small churches were founded, including the original St Mary Steps and St Olave's. Saint Nicholas Priory was built some time after 1087. The surviving part of this small Benedictine house has been restored as one of Exeter's first rate city museums. Part of St Katherine's Priory (circa 1160) survives in Polsloe off St Katherine's Road.

These buildings were overshadowed by the new Norman cathedral. Building in Beer stone, the beautiful white limestone from East Devon which also features in the present cathedral, the Norman workmen began their task in 1112. Their great-grandsons completed it around 1200. Although the massive Norman transeptal towers (unique in England) remain, the rest of this building is obscured by the Gothic cathedral seen

today. This was an equally long project, begun in 1275 and completed in 1360-70.

Exeter maintained its position as a commercial and industrial as well as a religious centre. One of the most significant developments was the reclaiming of Exe Island during the twelfth century. Leats were cut to drain the marshy land. The leats powered mills, including tucking (fulling) mills, tanneries and corn mills, helping to make Exeter one of England's leading cloth towns by 1200 – a position it retained until the eighteenth century.

As further evidence of civic pride and prosperity, the early medieval Guildhall was rebuilt in 1468 and the magnificent portico added in 1592. The Guildhall is thus one of the oldest municipal buildings in England still in use. Given Exeter's position in the woollen industry, the Guild of Weavers, Fullers and Shearmen became one of the city's most powerful companies, overshadowing the other guilds of barbers, cappers, butchers, brewers, bakers, cordwainers (shoemakers), smiths, cutlers and skinners. Tuckers Hall (i.e. fullers' hall) still stands in Fore Street and the Guild of Weavers, Fullers and Shearmen continues. Representatives of the Guild take part in civic events in their green gowns and caps.

In 1205 King John granted Exeter a charter allowing it to elect its own mayor annually. Up till then it was governed by two portreeves nominated by the Earl of Devon. Only London and Winchester had mayors at this time. The honour was doubled in 2002, when Elizabeth II granted Exeter a Lord Mayor.

Alured de Porta had the unique and unpleasant distinction for an Exeter Mayor of being hanged as a felon in 1285. He was implicated in the murder of Walter Lechlade, a precentor of the cathedral. Such was the rancour surrounding this murder that Bishop Quivel appealed to King Edward I, who judged the case at Rougemont and passed sentence of death on de Porta and four accomplices – although the actual murderers had not been discovered.

Bishop Quivel subsequently had the Cathedral Close walled off from the city, just as Rougemont was. Access, as at Lincoln, York and later Salisbury, was to be through gates that were locked at night.

A very real fear of plague might be another reason for Bishop Quivel's wish to keep the city at bay. In 1234, two thirds of Exeter's population had died of plague. The Black Death struck Europe in 1348-49 and it seemed that Armageddon was nigh, with half the population of the Continent

Opposite: Rougemont Castle gatehouse, a print published in 1822

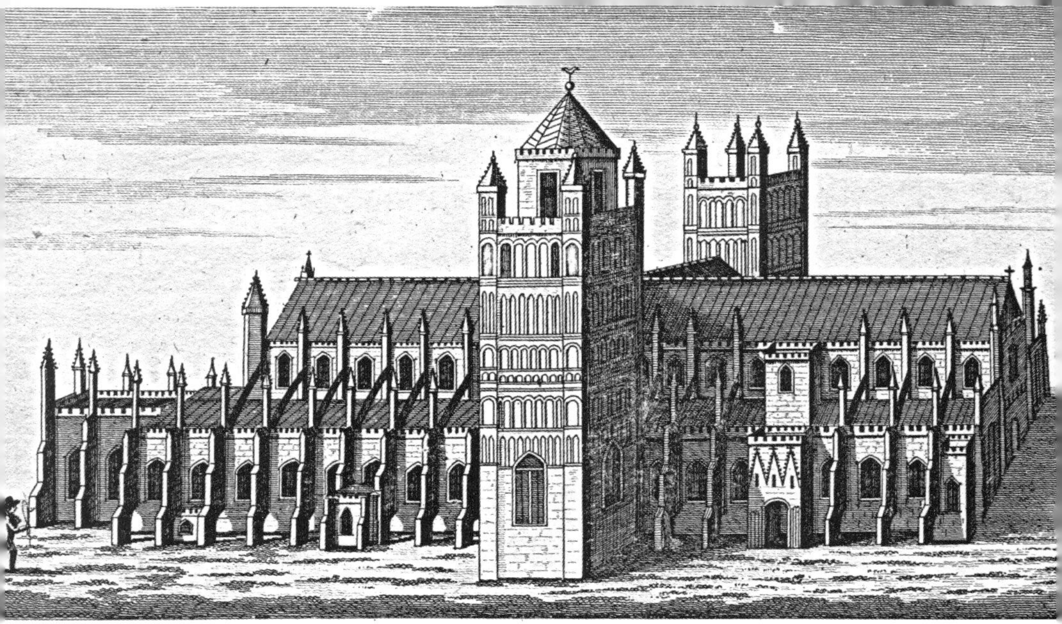

The Cathedral, a print dating from 1779

wiped out. Exeter lost half or more of its 3000 citizens. Many of the cathedral builders succumbed, which partly explains why the building took so long to finish.

From its earliest days, roads converged on Exeter. Traffic from the west was obliged to cross the Exe. Richard Hooker (Exeter's first historian) tells us of 'certain clappers of timber which served for men to pass over on foot' before the medieval stone bridge was built. Horses and carts must have forded the river or used a ferry. This practice appears to have continued. A drawing by Willem Schellinks of the medieval stone Exe Bridge in 1662 shows horsemen and packhorses fording the river.

The first definite evidence of a stone bridge over the Exe at Exeter dates from 1196, when 'a chaplain of the bridge' was mentioned. Nicholas Gervase, a wealthy Exeter merchant and his son Walter (Mayor 1236-38), moved by the loss of life on the old ford and footbridge, were chiefly responsible for completing Exe Bridge in 1238. Walter Gervase raised 10,000 marks to finish the bridge and endow it with enough funds for its perpetual repair. Nicholas and his wife were buried at St Edmund's chapel on the bridge. They are remembered in Gervase Avenue, Exeter.

This bridge probably began just outside the West Gate, at the foot of Stepcote Hill. A reproduction of a seventeenth century map of Exeter on display in the Devon Record Office gives a vivid impression of how the city was centred on the river. It shows that Exe Bridge stretched over what was then and for centuries after waterlogged marsh, but is now drained, culverted and built over. This low-lying land by Exe Bridge, known as Bonhay, Exe Island, Millhay and Shilhay, was then a string of islands. Split into leats, the river drove a series of mills – Bonhay, Cucking Stool, Lower and Cricklepit Mills. (At Cricklepit, the inner waterwheel has been restored to drive the stones, whilst the external wheel turns, but is unattached. It is planned to open Cricklepit Mill in March 2008). Cloth produced here was hung out to dry on racks and stretched by tenterhooks, as shown in early maps – and remembered in the name Rack Street.

Alphington Road, Cowick Street and Okehampton Road radiated out from the St Thomas end of medieval Exe Bridge, just as they do today. At the Exeter end, traffic from all directions was similarly funnelled down to the bridge. There was no Bonhay Road. Traffic for Cowley Bridge and North Devon used North Road by the old North Gate – and continued to do so to the building of North Road Bridge in 1834 and well beyond.

With an estimated span of two hundred metres, medieval Exe Bridge probably had eighteen arches. It was five metres wide and had a 3.5 metre carriageway. Eight and a half arches can be seen today on what is now dry land, though the remains of St Edmund's Church are not original. They date only from the 1830s. The houses that stood on the arches in Victorian paintings were demolished in 1881.

As well as being a focus for roads, Exeter was a sea port, but major problems arose concerning the use of the Exe. The Courtenay family, Earls of Devon, owned the manor of Topsham and the marshy ground (Exe Island) between Topsham and Exeter. They were thus in a position to control the river. Isabella de Fortibus, Countess of Devon in her own right, made two weirs across the Exe to drive her mill at the manor of Topsham in 1284.

Isabella, who is remembered in the name Countess Wear, left a ten metre gap between the weirs to permit ships to sail on to Exeter, but the astute Hugh de Courtenay, who succeeded to her title and possessions, stopped up the gap about 1311. This prevented ships and boats from reaching Exeter at all and forced them to unload at Hugh's quay at Topsham. Some of the cargoes were stored in his cellars, others, such as the stone used in Exeter Cathedral, were carted up the Topsham Road, no doubt to his considerable profit.

Topsham thus became a rival port to Exeter. Topsham merchants built their maritime trade at Exeter's expense, developing a business network with the Continent. Although it has been within the city boundaries since 1966, Topsham, which received its charter in 1257 from Henry III, was very much a separate entity and still retains its character and identity.

The Guildhall, rebuilt 1468, its portico dating from 1592, here seen as it was in 1829

Exeter sent many petitions to successive kings to remedy the situation created by the weirs. For example, in 1461 the city authorities wrote that the Countess of Devon had 'made a great nuisance by erecting a weare… salmon fishing is now destroyed on this side. Boats and vessels laden with wine and merchandise cannot come up.' All this was to no avail until the powerful and very well connected Courtenays fell from favour in 1538, as we shall see in the next chapter.

Meanwhile, the city and the Courtenays took opposing sides in the Wars of the Roses, Exeter favouring the Lancastrian cause, the Courtenays the Yorkists. In 1470, Exeter withstood a twelve day siege by Sir William Courtenay.

As Exeter recovered from the ravages of the Black Death during the fifteenth century and the wool trade brought renewed prosperity, most of the central churches were rebuilt in coarse red Heavitree sandstone. Other notable buildings from this period include Wynard's Hospital, built in 1435 by the Recorder of Exeter, William Wynard, and what is now the White Hart in South Street. This was possibly Wynard's own house and later became the Blue Boar. It has a richly carved ceiling and fire-place. Other fifteenth century houses include two at the foot of Stepcote Hill, numbers 46 and 47 in High Street and several in North Street.

3 Tudor Exeter

Although the Wars of the Roses ended with Henry Tudor's victory against Richard III at Bosworth in 1485 and Tudor was crowned Henry VII, civil unrest simmered on in England. Exeter was menaced twice in 1497. In the spring, a large body of Cornishmen rebelled against taxes levied by Henry VII to fight the Scots – a war the Cornish considered had nothing to do with them. On their way up to London, the Cornish captains were allowed to pass through Exeter, but their men were obliged to detour around the city walls. The Cornish force marched on, but was defeated at Blackheath near London. Anti-war protests are nothing new.

Later in 1497 Perkin Warbeck attacked Exeter with 4-5000 men. Warbeck was a pretender to the throne who claimed to be the Duke of York, the younger of the two princes who had mysteriously disappeared from the Tower of London during Richard III's reign. Warbeck's forces attempted to burn Exeter's North Gate, and then broke through the East Gate. Exonians counter-attacked and drove Warbeck back up the High Street. Having lost 400 men at Exeter, he retreated to Taunton and surrendered to King Henry, who marched the prisoners back to Exeter, where he had the leaders hung, drawn and quartered. Henry was more lenient with the lesser rebels, staging a grand pardon outside the Exeter Treasurer's House. The prisoners, with nooses around their necks were obliged to sue for mercy, which Henry granted.

In recognition for Exeter's loyal service, the king presented the city with his sword and cap of maintenance. He commanded these should be carried by the Mayor on all public occasions 'from the time being for ever'. The tradition continues.

The city was further honoured in 1588, when Queen Elizabeth wrote to her 'ever faithful' Exeter in recognition of its loyal support in paying towards the cost of supplying three ships to fight the Spanish Armada. *Semper fidelis* ('ever faithful') was adopted as Exeter's motto.

Exeter was not immune from the religious turmoil of the sixteenth century. In 1531 Exeter schoolmaster Thomas Benet, inspired by Martin Luther's radical new ideas, posted notices around the city that 'the Pope is the Antichrist and we ought to worship God not the saints'. He refused to recant and was burnt as a heretic at Livery Dole in 1532.

Meanwhile, matters took a very different turn. Henry VIII kick-started the English Reformation, breaking with Rome, divorcing Catherine of Aragon and declaring himself Head of the Church of England. He also dissolved the monasteries between 1536 and 1540. St Nicholas Priory was partly demolished in 1536; the masonry was used to repair Exe Bridge and to build a new wool market in South Street. Polsloe Priory with its fourteen nuns was dissolved in 1538, along with Exeter's two friaries. John Hull of Larkbeare obtained the land owned by the Grey Friars and Lord John Russell was appointed to oversee the Reformation in Devon. Russell was granted the Dominican house near the Cathedral, which he called Bedford House.

Religious strife was again unleashed in 1549, when Edward VI's government imposed a reformed church service in English, with new rituals and prayer book. Many people in the devout and conservative west were deeply attached to the Catholic Mass in Latin. The Cornish additionally resented the imposition of an English service, for many spoke Cornish – English was a foreign language.

Again, Cornishmen marched east. Some three thousand joined a force of like-minded prayer book rebels who had assembled at Sampford Courtenay north of Okehampton. Marching on Exeter, the rebels found Mayor John Blackaller resolved not to surrender the city, key to control of the west.

On 2 July 1549, they besieged Exeter, where loyalties were divided. Catholics within the city did not open Exeter's gates, perhaps from fear of looting, perhaps from fear of their Protestant neighbours and the approaching royal forces under Lord John Russell. Although the rebels did not succeed in their siege, they captured St Sidwell's church outside the walls and held prisoners in the tower. One was Sir Walter Raleigh senior, who had scolded an old lady for carrying a rosary.

Russell defeated the rebels in three battles in East Devon and relieved Exeter on 6 August, where the citizens had been reduced to eating horse meat and even horse fodder. He immediately set about rewarding his allies and punishing his foes, including Robert Welshe, the vicar of St Thomas. Welshe was a Cornishman and sympathised with the rebels, though he had persuaded them not to attempt burning Exeter. This did not save him from Russell. He was hanged from his own church tower, dressed in his Roman vestments, carrying his rosary 'and other popish trash'. His tarred body hung there for four years, until Queen Mary's reign.

Miles Coverdale, who translated the Bible into English, was Russell's chaplain during the campaign, which concluded with the ringleaders' executions. Coverdale became bishop of Exeter in 1551. Two years later, he was preaching in the cathedral when news arrived that devoutly Catholic Mary had succeeded her Protestant half-brother, Edward VI, as monarch. Prudently, Coverdale stopped preaching and fled the country.

Mary re-imposed Catholicism on England and it was the turn of Protestants to suffer. In 1557, Agnes Prest denied the doctrine of transubstantiation and was burnt at the stake in Southernhay. She and Thomas Benet are commemorated with a tall obelisk in Denmark Road.

Elizabeth became queen in 1558. She re-imposed the Protestant faith and Catholicism was again suppressed. Exeter gained a Catholic martyr in 1599. James Dowdall denied the Queen's spiritual ascendancy and was hung, drawn and quartered at Rougemont.

The violent religious obsessions of the sixteenth century left a deep mark on Exeter. Not surprisingly, the walls and gates were maintained. John Hooker, Exeter's Tudor historian, described how the porters 'must every night shut and make fast the City's Gates at Ten of the Clock at Night in the Summer and Nine of the Clock in Winter; and must open the said Gates at Four of the Clock in the Morning in Summer and Five of the Clock in Winter...' and 'forthwith close and make fast the Gates' in the event of any 'Tumults, Uproars, Escapes of Prisoners, Firing of Houses...'

The sense of separateness induced by strong defences was underscored in 1537 when Exeter became a county in its own right, separate from Devon, electing its own Sheriff. This recognised Exeter's economic importance as Tudor England's fifth city, only exceeded in wealth and population by London, Norwich, Bristol and Newcastle. Exeter did not become part of Devon again until local government reorganization in 1972.

In 1550 Edward VI granted Exe Island to Exeter in recognition of the city's defence against the Prayer Book rebels the year before. He was able to do this because Exe Island and adjoining parts of the river had been seized from Henry Courtenay in 1538 by King Henry VIII. The king accused Courtenay, his former favourite, of treason and he was (of course) beheaded.

Exeter's city fathers were determined that maritime trade should be revived. However, attempts to break down the weirs built by the Courtenays and clear the Exe of accumulated silt failed to achieve their purpose of opening it to shipping. A new quay was therefore built in 1565 and a canal was cut between 1564 and 1567 by John Trewe. This was the first canal in Britain to use pound locks – a fact commemorated, like many developments in history, in the name of an inn, The Double Locks.

Unfortunately, Trewe's scheme was not bold or far reaching enough and only the smallest ships could make Exeter Quay at high tide. Despite further improvements to the canal in 1670, a large portion of Exeter's seaborne trade continued to be handled at Topsham until the extension of the canal to Turf in 1826, which included the construction of a huge lock capable of taking ships with a three metre draught.

Tudor Exeter produced three men who made a mark on national history. Thomas Bodley was born the son of an Exeter merchant in 1545. Scholar and diplomat, Bodley devoted his later years to re-founding Oxford University's library, which had been wrecked in Edward VI's turbulent reign. The library was named the Bodleian in 1604.

The Bodleys were Puritans who had found refuge in Protestant Geneva during the persecutions of Queen Mary's reign. Accompanying them was the young Nicholas Hilliard, the son of an Exeter goldsmith, who became a close friend of Thomas Bodley. Hilliard was a highly talented artist. Appointed limner and goldsmith to Elizabeth I at the age of only 24, he became one of the first great painters of miniature portraits.

The imposing statue of Richard Hooker was erected on the Cathedral Green in 1907. Richard, nephew of the historian John Hooker already quoted, was born in Heavitree about 1553 and wrote a famous defence of the Elizabethan Church of England, officially the established religion, but far from secure. In an intolerant age, Hooker urged much needed charity and tolerance towards Catholics and Calvinists. His stately literary style was also greatly admired.

4 Stuart Exeter

Richard Hooker was ahead of his time. Seventeenth century England witnessed continued religious tension, which did a great deal to ignite and fuel the Civil War. Loyalty to King Charles I or Parliament was a fraught and complex matter for many people, not least in Devon where the issue has recently been analysed by historian Mark Stoyle (see Bibliography). As in 1549 at the time of the Prayer Book Rebellion, Exeter's loyalties were sharply divided. Again, the main cleavage was along religious lines. The Established Church, especially the Dean and Chapter, were Royalist, as were some of the leading merchants. However, there was also a powerful Puritan and Dissenting element in Exeter, including several leading citizens, who identified strongly with Parliament.

When war broke out in 1642, a special watch was maintained at Exeter by thirty-two chosen citizens. Ammunition and corn was stockpiled; the city's walls were surveyed and repaired and six guns mounted along them – a meagre defence for the 2.5km circuit.

Although the Royalist general, Sir Ralph Hopton, succeeded in securing most of the south-west for Charles, he was defeated at Laira, just outside staunchly Parliamentarian Plymouth. Defeated again at Modbury in the South Hams, Hopton marched on Exeter at the end of 1642 and called upon it to surrender. Mayor Christopher Clark refused. Short of supplies for a prolonged siege, Hopton wisely withdrew.

Purging the administration of Royalists, the city fathers ordered more ammunition and formed volunteers into companies to defend the walls and garrison the castle. Ditches were deepened and strengthened and drawbridges placed on the city gates. To give a clear field of fire, houses near the city walls were demolished.

Having won a victory at Stratton on the Cornish border, the Royalist forces returned to Exeter under Sir John Berkeley and began their siege on 19 June, 1643. Prince Maurice reinforced Berkeley in late August and the city surrendered after a total of eleven weeks' siege on 4 September.

Sir John Berkeley governed Exeter under the new Royalist regime, which lasted until April 1646, making the city King Charles' headquarters in the west and levying a hefty £40 per week from it for the war effort. A mint was established to coin money for Royalist soldiers.

In 1644, the Queen left Oxford, which was threatened by Parliament, and found refuge in Exeter. Here, she gave birth to Princess Henrietta, who was christened in the Cathedral. A new font was made for the occasion, which is the one seen today.

After Parliament's victory at Naseby, 14 June 1645, the tide turned irrevocably against King Charles. Late in the year, Fairfax and Cromwell attempted to surround Exeter. Powderham, the Courtenay seat, held out against them. There was a bloody skirmish at Powderham church in which a Roundhead force was besieged for three hours by a combined party of Royalists from Exeter and Powderham Castle. Eventually, all the soldiers withdrew.

In January 1646 the campaign was pressed deeper into Devon and the Royalists were defeated at Bovey Tracey and Dartmouth. The Parliamentarian commanders returned to Exeter, where the siege continued.

Keeping up the pressure on Exeter, Fairfax marched to Torrington in North Devon, where he defeated Hopton on 16 February.

Returning again to besiege Exeter, Fairfax called on Sir John Berkeley to admit defeat. Berkeley saw the sense of this and an honourable surrender was negotiated for 13 April 1646. 'The governor, together with all lords, clergymen, gentlemen, captains, officers, troopers and common soldiers shall march out of the city…with their horses, full arms, bag and baggage, and their goods, colours flying, drums beating, matches lighted and full bandoliers…'

The city in 1771. Notice the cloth-drying racks on the right of the picture

Moreover, it was agreed that there would be no plundering and that Princess Henrietta and her household should be allowed to go free, with their belongings. It was also agreed that those symbols of Royalism, the Cathedral and the parish churches, should not be damaged or plundered in any way.

However, that last clause was soon broken in an outbreak of iconoclastic fervour – or possibly destructive malice. Windows in the Cathedral were smashed and many statues beheaded. The gates of the Close were torn down. Clergymen were driven from their homes; the Chapter House and Bishop's Palace were used as stables.

Parliamentarian soldiers swaggered through the streets of Exeter with pipes looted from the Cathedral's organ 'piping in a scornful and contemptuous manner'. One group is said to have scoffed at the choristers: 'Boys we have spoilt your trade; you must go and sing hot pudding pies!'

Less crude, but nonetheless telling affronts were offered by the authorities. A cloth hall was built in the Cathedral's cloisters during the Protectorate – this can still be readily discerned in the wooden pillars there. Meanwhile, the Cathedral was divided by a brick wall to allow the Presbyterians to worship in one half and the Congregationalist Independents in the other. Presumably, there was no love lost between these two Christian groups.

Prominent citizens who had supported the vanquished Royalist cause were heavily fined for their 'delinquency'. Roger Mallock, one of the richest merchants, was fined nearly £1600 and Robert Walker nearly £900 – huge sums in the money of the time.

Between 1646 and the Restoration in 1660, Exeter was under military occupation. Not only was it strategically important, but western Royalists hoped to stage a rising and recapture it. Had they done so, they would certainly have found supporters within the city. Post-war Exeter was not a contented place. Aside from structural damage, the war had done immense harm to Exeter's trade and left the city with a £14,000 debt.

The proclamation of Charles II's accession in 1660 was greeted with some rejoicing in Exeter. A hogshead of claret was fixed to each of the city's three public conduits – perhaps some regarded that as symbolic of the new era of self-indulgence. Meanwhile, the depredations of war were made good and Southernhay and Northernhay planted with elms. The cloth hall in the cloisters was closed and converted into a music school and the brick wall dividing the Cathedral torn down. In 1665 the organ, vandalised by Puritan zealots, was restored.

In 1670 Charles II visited Exeter. He was given £500 and he knighted the Mayor. Charles presented the city with a portrait of his recently deceased sister, affectionately known as 'Minette' – the Princess Henrietta who had been born in Exeter in 1644. This now hangs in the Guildhall with several other royal portraits.

At the time of Charles' visit, Exeter was recovering its lost prosperity. This was aided by the extension and deepening of the canal to Topsham in 1676. Exeter's Custom House was built in 1680 to deal with considerably increased business at the Quay.

Charles was succeeded by his openly Catholic brother, James II, in 1685. The attempt by the Protestant Duke of Monmouth (one of Charles's thirteen illegitimate children) to take the throne from his uncle found widespread support in the West Country, not least among the traditionally Puritan clothing workers of East Devon. After Monmouth's defeat at the Battle of Sedgemoor (5 July 1685), the infamous Judge Jeffreys held one of his 'Bloody Assizes' at Exeter's Guildhall to try local rebels. Some were executed at Heavitree, others transported, flogged or fined.

In November 1688, William of Orange landed at Brixham. This Dutch pretender led his forces into Exeter under the banner GOD AND THE PROTESTANT RELIGION on his way to seize power. He received a wary reception at first, which is hardly surprising with the Bloody Assize fresh in Exonians' memories. A plaque by the remains of the West Gate in West Street commemorates William's triumphal entry. William, an experienced besieger of cities, was not impressed by Exeter's defences: 'I could take this city with baked apples,' he jibed.

Happily, there was no renewal of the Civil Wars and William enjoyed a bloodless coup. Exeter could again concentrate on business, above all the woollen trade, though trade with Spain, Portugal and Italy also flourished. Portuguese and Spanish wine founded more than one merchant's fortune in Exeter.

Opposite: The North tower of the Cathedral; from The beauties of England and Wales, *one of the many topograpical collections of the Regency period*

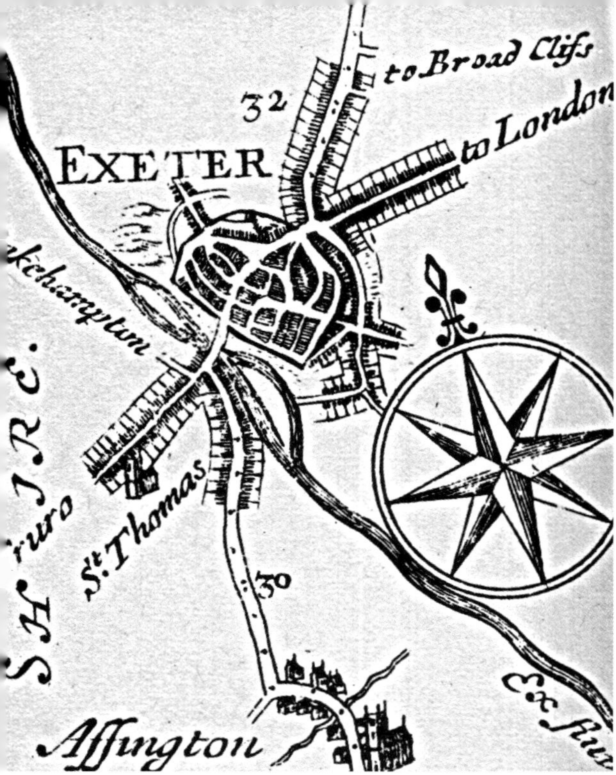

The city as it was in 1675, twenty years before Celia Fiennes and Daniel Defoe made their comments. It is still largely contained within the Roman walls, with ribbon development along the main roads – which were no better than modern rural bridleways, fit for trains of packhorses rather than wheeled traffic. The bulk of trade was carried by water rather than by road

In 1681, the woollen serge shipped annually from Exeter and Topsham represented one sixth of the English woollen market. Often the cloth went direct to the Netherlands. Dutch bricks frequently came back as ballast on the return trip and some of these can be seen in the so called 'Dutch' houses on Topsham's tasteful Strand, including the Museum, number 25.

Indeed, Topsham provides the most visible evidence of the wealth the wool trade brought. Between about 1660 and 1730 the town was at its zenith and was virtually rebuilt. It 'can boast the most attractive street of mercantile houses anywhere in England,' according to buildings historian John Thorp.

At the turn of the eighteenth century, Exeter was also at the height of its prosperity, one of the largest cities in England with a population of 13,000. Indefatigable travel writers Daniel Defoe and Celia Fiennes have left vivid portraits of the city at this time.

Defoe noted 'the city drives a very great correspondence with Holland. He approved of Exeter because it 'is large, rich, beautiful, populous' and also because ''tis full of gentry and good company, yet full of trade and manufactures also… The serge market held here every week is very worth a stranger seeing and next to the Brigg Market in Leeds in Yorkshire, is the greatest in England. The people assured me that at this market is generally sold from sixty, seventy to eighty and sometimes a hundred thousand pounds value of serges in a week.'

For Celia Fiennes Exeter was 'a town very well built, the streets are well pitched, spacious noble streets, and a vast trade is carried on... The whole town and country is employed for at least twenty miles round in spinning, weaving, dressing and scouring, fulling and drying of the serges.'

Fiennes was also impressed by Exeter's commerce, its 'Exchange full of shops' and 'several markets' and claimed it 'does exceedingly resemble London' – which was probably meant as a compliment. She also described how the Exe was diverted into leats to drive mills and how Exonians 'catch the salmon as they leap with spears'.

5 Georgian Exeter

Wealth created by the wool trade was used by enterprising Exeter businessmen in other commercial ventures, notably banking. John Baring, who came to Exeter in 1717 from Germany, founded a merchant banking dynasty. Later established in London, Baring Brothers became internationally renowned. Baring's fellow German émigré, Sir John Duntze, was a partner in the Exeter Bank, the earliest of several banks established in the city, whilst 'a serge merchant of great respectability', Joshua Williams, founded the General Bank in 1792.

As well as their strong connections with the wool trade, the founders of Exeter's early banks were notable for being, almost to a man, Nonconformists. Excluded from much of public life, from the professions and from the ancient universities, talented Nonconformists turned to business. Georgian Exeter had strong and influential communities of Presbyterians, Baptists and Quakers.

Nonetheless, Nonconformists, especially the Wesleyans, sometimes had difficulties in Exeter. According to *The London Post* of 1745:

> In Exeter the Methodists had a meeting house behind the Guildhall... the mob gathered at the door and pelted those who entered with potatoes, mud and dung. On coming out, the congregation were all beaten, without exception; many were trampled underfoot; many fled without their hats and wigs.

As Exeter was the third city in England to have a newspaper, daily events in the city have been particularly well recorded. *The Exeter Post Man* first appeared in 1704, followed by *The Exeter Post Boy* in 1707 and *The Exeter Mercury* in 1714.

Houses near the South Gate in the early nineteenth century, showing an inn and, apparently, a laundry

Although modernising in several ways, Georgian Exeter retained a largely medieval appearance behind its ancient walls. Its narrow streets and many steep gradients were poorly suited to wheeled traffic, which was virtually unknown in the West Country before 1750, but which soon became common with the construction of turnpike roads.

Devon gained its first turnpike trust in 1751. Thirty-one more trusts followed in the county, doing more than anything else to open Devon to the outside world by widening, straightening and maintaining roads.

Road improvements, combined with better coaches and the improved facilities offered by coaching inns, cut the Exeter to London journey from the four days recorded in 1658 to two days in the 1750s. However, the first mail coaches made the journey in only twenty-four hours in 1785 and averaged nine miles per hour, nearly 15km/h. Speed indeed!

Traffic faced severe problems in Exeter, the hub of Devon's road network. It was forced to funnel slowly through the city's four gates. These had served their turn in many attacks and sieges, but as King William III had contemptuously pointed out in 1688, they could not stand against modern artillery. Moreover, the threat of civil war had receded greatly. Demolition seemed the obvious course and Exeter's North Gate was the first to go in 1769. East Gate came down in 1784, West Gate in 1815 and South Gate in 1819. The destruction of South Gate must have delighted the debtors kept imprisoned in the upper room. This was known as 'the shoe' as prisoners begged for alms by lowering a shoe on a string – reputedly the origin of 'living on a shoestring'.

Increased coaching traffic led the Exeter Turnpike Trust to build a bridge at Countess Wear. Thomas Parker of Topsham completed it in 1774 to traditional design. Countess Wear Bridge has lasted well. It was widened in 1938 to 13.5 metres to carry the Exeter bypass. Before the M5 was opened, it carried up to 60,000 vehicles per day. Now, it is part of the A379 and still busy.

The Exeter Turnpike Trust also built a new Exe Bridge in 1773, but this washed away only two years later. A replacement bridge, laid on solid rock, was completed in 1778. It cost £30,000 and was 7.5 metres wide.

Another artist's view of the South Gate, which was demolished in 1819

Typical of the era, it had three fine arches and an elegant parapet, as surviving drawings and later photographs show.

A letter to the *Exeter Flying Post* of 1772 said the new turnpike roads had brought 'families of Fortune and Distinction' to settle in Exeter, which was certainly becoming more sophisticated, with rudimentary street lights by 1768, pavements to its main streets from 1778 and its first sewers in 1807. Exeter was also expanding with well-proportioned new houses. These were often in the fashionable Palladian style, notable for its national rather than local flavour. In 1773 Bedford Circus was built, with a theatre incorporated in 1787.

Unfortunately, Bedford Circus was badly damaged in the 1942 Blitz. Subsequently (and controversially) it was demolished. However, many fine Georgian buildings in locally made red brick survive in Exeter. Between them, local builders William Hooper and Matthew Nosworthy developed Southernhay, Barnfield Crescent and Colleton Crescent (overlooking the Quay) in similar style during the closing years of the eighteenth and the early years of the nineteenth centuries. This attractive building tradition continued with Pennsylvania in the 1820s.

Pennsylvania shortly around 1830, with a superb view over the city

The Subscription Rooms (a public assembly rooms, including a ballroom) and in the background the New London Inn, about 1830

Exeter's position as an up-market retreat from London and as a retirement centre was boosted by the Napoleonic Wars. With foreign travel all but impossible, wealthy English people patronised the English coast and provincial towns. One such was travel writer Richard Ford, who boasted to his friends that Exeter, his new home, was 'quite a capital, abounding in all that London has, except for its fog and smoke.' Similar remarks can be heard today.

Turnpike roads and much faster coaches had brought London closer to Exeter, which developed as a coaching centre with a great array of inns and stables, as well as England's first hotel, established in 1770. This became the Royal Clarence Hotel in 1827, when patronised by the Duchess of Clarence. It has now been re-named The Abode Exeter.

In 1831, up to seventy passenger coaches left Exeter daily. The Royal Mail quit the New London Inn in Exeter at 9.45am and reached London at 6.30am the next day. The fare for this gruelling journey was 35 shillings outside or £3 10s inside the coach.

Indefatigable coach traveller Charles Dickens took the coach to Exeter in 1835 to report the hustings for the *Morning Chronicle*. This experience is said to have inspired the Eatanswill elections in *Pickwick Papers*, whilst the somnolent Fat Boy was based on a character at Exeter's Turk's Head.

A further link between Dickens and Exeter was the author's infuriating and financially incorrigible father, the model it is said for Mr Micawber. Dickens hid his Aged Parent away from publicity and creditors at Mile End Cottage in Alphington. Dickens would have first arrived just after the New North Road was built in 1833. Its magnificent iron bridge (1834) was made at Russell and Brown's Blaina Iron Works, Monmouthshire, as proudly announced on the central arch. Between 1835 and 1840, Queen Street was extended over a viaduct to meet North Road.

Exeter's wool trade, for centuries the foundation of its wealth, did not benefit greatly from turnpike roads. Out-competed by the new industrial centres of Northern England, which benefited from proximity to the coalfields, Devon's wool industry declined during the eighteenth century. It was all but strangled during the long Napoleonic War blockades.

Despite this, Exeter grew apace. Its population doubled between 1800 and 1840. Trade was resilient and the Quay at its busiest around 1830, every berth packed with sailing vessels. In response, the canal was extended in 1826 and the canal basin was enlarged in 1830.

In 1840, *Alert* became the first steamship to use the Exeter Ship Canal and dock in the new basin. According to *Trewman's Exeter Flying Post* 'She is built of iron and a fine vessel of her class. She is 90 feet in length, about 23 feet in width and of 30 horse power. She is 22 tons burden and draws 2½ feet of water.'

Two massive warehouses were built on the Quay in 1834-35 to handle a wide range of cargoes, including corn, timber, coal and barites, a mineral mined in Devon. Although put to new uses, these warehouses still dominate the Quay and featured in the BBC's maritime drama *The Onedin Line*, in which Exeter Quay represented Victorian Liverpool.

Like Liverpool, Exeter was grossly overcrowded. The first Ordnance Survey map of Exeter was made in 1809 (see Bibliography) and shows the city still largely confined within its medieval walls, covering a mere one square kilometre. However, Exeter and its working class suburb of St Thomas counted 20,000 people, packed into just over 3000 houses. This meant many houses were subdivided into cramped tenements.

Overcrowding and primitive sanitation led to major public health problems. Exeter's cholera epidemic of 1832-33 claimed 438 victims in sombre contrast to the city's progress in buildings and transport. Afterwards, a programme of public health improvements was driven forward. Many courts and alleyways were opened to improve ventilation. The whole city was sewered at the cost of £80,000. Longbrook and the charming Shitbrook, previously used as open sewers, were culverted.

A new waterworks was built to draw water from the Exe a mile upriver from the pollution of the Quay – it had previously been common practice to scoop drinking water out of the river in buckets wherever convenient. Market stalls were cleared from Exeter's crowded streets and put into two purpose-built market halls, whilst the cattle market was moved from heavily populated Bartholomew Street to Bonhay.

6 Victorian Exeter

The prosperity of Exeter's Quay was suddenly and dramatically undermined when the railway arrived in Exeter in 1844 from Bristol. It was extended to Plymouth in 1848. Daniel Gooch, assistant to Chief Engineer IK Brunel, managed a non-stop journey to Paddington of only 4 hours 26 minutes. Averaging 67km/h, this was unparalleled for sustained high-speed running at the time and a triumph for Brunel's broad gauge system. Standard journey times to London were soon reduced to a mere five hours, including stops, making them the fastest train journeys in the world, a quarter the time taken by the coach.

The railway's arrival announced a new era for Exeter. However, the brilliant Brunel overreached himself with his attempted Atmospheric Railway. Doubting the capacity of conventional locomotives to cope with steep gradients (up to 1 in 36) west of Exeter, Brunel looked to atmospheric traction for a radical solution. Stationary steam engines built at intervals along the track would replace locomotives. These engines would create a vacuum in a central pipe that ran between the rails and was joined to the train by a hinged piston, thus drawing it along by atmospheric pressure. The concept of generating power outside the train and thus reducing its weight dramatically was theoretically sound and anticipated electrification by a century.

Not only would atmospheric traction help trains cope with stiff gradients, it would also be cleaner and quieter. Brunel was fascinated with the apparent potential of this technology, which had been applied with some success on short railway lines elsewhere.

The atmospheric system only operated from September 1847 to June 1848 between Exeter and Newton Abbot. It never reached Totnes, although the pipes were laid. At the beginning, its performance was promising indeed. Speeds of over 95km/h were attained, but in the winter the all-important leather flap valve, which sealed the continuous slot along the top of the vacuum pipe, often froze. Rats gnawed it and the salt air completed its destruction. Costly repairs were demanded, and the pumping houses used far more fuel than expected.

On a main line, the atmospheric system suffered from other innate difficulties that were never solved – and perhaps never could have been solved. Uncoupling locomotives and coupling carriages with atmospheric pistons at Exeter was time-consuming and labour-intensive. Making junctions with other railway lines and accommodating level crossings presented major challenges. Brunel courageously admitted his error of judgement. He introduced locomotives at Exeter forthwith, scrapping the project that had caught his imagination.

Despite this setback, the railways centred on Exeter prospered, improving communications within Devon out of all recognition and giving many Exonians employment, both directly and indirectly. Exeter was connected by rail to Crediton in 1851 and Barnstaple in 1854. The 1860 link to Yeovil (and thus the shorter southern route to London) led directly to building the branch line to Exmouth in 1861.

The Exmouth line, which offered Exonians a day trip to the seaside, was followed by the Exe Valley Line in 1885. The Okehampton and Tavistock route to Plymouth was completed in 1890 and the Teign Valley Line in 1903.

Victorian Exeter became a railway centre, just as it had previously been a road and coaching centre. There was no alternative but to adopt London time (GMT), because all British trains ran on standard London time. Being over three degrees longitude west of London, Exeter's clocks were fourteen minutes behind those in the capital in the pre-railway era because they (like the London clocks) were set to local time, which depended upon the position of the sun. Only in 1880 was GMT was imposed all over Britain. Today, we take it entirely for granted.

With its excellent railway connections, Exeter became an even more popular excursion centre than it had been during the coaching era. In addition to its many historic buildings, the city gained a new church on Mount Dinham. St Michael and All Angels, completed in 1868, has a 67 metre tall spire (now floodlit).

Exeter also gained the Royal Albert Memorial Museum in 1869. Built in French Gothic style, this imposing building incorporated a library, reading room, science classes and a school of art after a fashion the high-minded Prince Albert would have approved. It remains an excellent free museum, with extensive local history collections.

To cater for visitors' more worldly needs, the mid-Victorian city had 148 inns, hotels and taverns. When, in 1872, new licensing laws required these to shut at 11pm, the good citizens responded with several nights of rioting.

The Cathedral Close, with St Mary Major on the right, and some attractive trees suitable for a genteel promenade

Although Exeter with its Cathedral Close provided part of the imaginary setting for Anthony Trollope's delightful *Barchester Chronicles*, with its bumbling bishops and unworldly wardens, the real Close was not invariably tranquil. Down to the end of the nineteenth century, Guy Fawkes' night was celebrated with great gusto outside the Cathedral, with a massive bonfire and fireworks. In 1867, Exeter's Mayor, fearing the celebrations were getting out of hand, summoned troops, who advanced on the crowd with fixed bayonets.

In 1887 fire engulfed the Theatre Royal after part of the scenery collapsed and was ignited by a broken gas mantle. Panic ensued as the audience rushed for the only exit – an inward facing door. 188 people died, many of asphyxiation.

A new Theatre Royal was built the following year, incorporating fire exits that opened outwards and a fire curtain to separate the audience from the stage. These safety improvements later became legal requirements in all theatres. Another positive result of this tragedy was the formation of Exeter's new City Fire Brigade.

Exeter saw its first motor car in 1897, when a Daimler was shown in a circus as a special attraction. Much impressed, a local mechanical engineer called Shepherd designed and built his own motor car in 1899.

Cars did not have such an immediate and dramatic impact on Exeter as railways had done. In 1904 the city had but twelve car owners, rising to 225 in 1912. Later in the twentieth century, cars were to dominate the city, its economy and planning, to a previously unimaginable extent. From 1300 cars in 1920, Exeter's car registrations rose to 4000 in 1947; 15,000 in 1960 and 40,000 in 2001, when 72% of households owned one or more cars.

7 Twentieth Century Exeter

We anticipate. Exeter at the start of the twentieth century was substantially smaller than today. Its population of 59,000 (compared with 110,000 in 2001) was much more concentrated in and around the old city. Certainly, the Exeter of 1900 had grown greatly, almost threefold from 1801 when its population was a mere 23,000. Ribbons of Victorian terraced streets clambered over Whipton and St Thomas – incorporated into Exeter in 1900 – as well as Heavitree, which officially became part of the city in 1913.

However, Exeter was no longer one of England's leading cities as it had been in the early eighteenth century. The industrial cities of the Midlands and North had quite eclipsed it in size, industry and wealth. Its relative position in 1900 was that of a provincial cathedral city, albeit with a history that made Birmingham, Leeds or Manchester look like upstarts.

Exeter was not altogether a backwater. 1905 brought three new developments: a new Exe Bridge, the first electric trams and the Buller statue. Exeter's first horse-drawn trams had been introduced in 1882, but the new century demanded something faster, cleaner and technically more advanced. The old tram tracks were re-employed; the twenty-two tram horses were sold off for £263 11s 6d and a new electricity works was built at the city basin to augment the first generating station of 1889.

Most significantly, the old three-arched Exe Bridge of 1778 was replaced with a modern bridge wide enough to take tram tracks and give the new machines an easy level crossing. Weighing 437 tonnes with a 112 tonne parapet, the new cast-iron single-span bridge was worthy of the twentieth century: 11 metres wide with footways of 2.5 metres.

Period postcards and photographs show a great crowd gathered on the flag bedecked bridge for the grand opening on 29 March, 1905. The Rifle Volunteers mounted a hundred-strong guard of honour, backed by the battalion band. Twenty-seven city police and twenty-five county constables kept order. Mayor Edwin C Perry included a special welcome in his speech to General Sir Redvers Buller, VC, the leading dignitary.

Mayor Perry and the flags were back in action a week later when he drove one of Exeter's first electric trams and opened the service to the public. On that first day, 4 April 1905, 7740 passengers travelled for two-pence each. By 8 July, a million tram journeys had been completed.

There were more flags, top hats, dignitaries and speeches than ever on 6 September, when the Buller statue was unveiled to the strains of 'Land of Hope and Glory'. The Lord Lieutenant of Devon described General Buller as 'Devon's most illustrious son of this period' in his speech.

Born at Downes, Crediton in 1839, Sir Redvers Buller had had an outstanding army career, culminating in command of the British forces in South Africa for the Second Boer War. Although his command was far from successful and he was rapidly replaced by General Frederick Roberts, Buller remained a hero in his home county. The four tonne bronze statue of Buller in full ceremonial uniform on his charger still stands proudly (and occasionally decorated with a traffic cone) at the junction of New North Road and Hele Road.

Despite the great excitement at their introduction, Exeter's trams had a short career. They lacked the versatility and range of motor buses. First introduced in 1929, motor buses replaced trams completely by 1931.

As for the 1905 Exe Bridge, it yielded eventually to vastly increased traffic and was replaced between 1969 and 1972 by the two massive utilitarian steel-beam slab-deck structures seen today. Each is bigger than the 1905 bridge, but both were dwarfed a few years later by the 695 metre long M5 Exe Viaduct, which was remarkable also for crossing the river's flood plain at a lower point than any attempted before in Exeter's many bridge building projects.

The Royal Albert Memorial College was also founded in first decade of the twentieth century. Using what are now the Phoenix Arts Centre premises in Gandy Street (built 1911), the College became the University of the South West in 1922. The Washington Singer Building was begun on the present university campus in 1927. More buildings followed on the old Streatham estate and Exeter became a full and independent university in 1955.

Many Exonians served and died in the First World War, as the war memorials in Northernhay and the Cathedral Green testify. However, the fighting did not impinge so directly and dramatically on the life of the city as the Second World War was to do.

Slum clearance in the interwar years focussed on the decayed West Quarter, where many children were glad of the 'farthing breakfast', a dole of bread, jam and cocoa paid for by public subscription. In this district, many old merchants' houses (which would now be listed buildings if they had survived) had been subdivided into overcrowded tenements. Hundreds of families were moved out to the Burnthouse Lane estate (nicknamed 'Siberia' for its relative remoteness) and Buddle Lane.

The growing number of cars in the 1920s led to jams in High Street and the first of Exeter's many bypasses was opened in 1927 through the Hoopern Valley. Exeter gained its first traffic lights in 1929 and its outer bypass in 1936. Other notable developments just before the war included the opening of St Loye's training centre for the disabled and Exeter Airport in 1937. In 1939, on the eve of war, the cattle market was moved from Bonhay Road to Alphington (it has since been moved again to Matford) and the once familiar processions of animals over Exe Bridge passed into history.

War came. Exeter Airport was requisitioned by the RAF and two squadrons were based there, fighting in the Battle of Britain, 1940. The Luftwaffe raided Exeter seventeen times between August 1940 and December 1942, but most of the destruction wrought by German bombs came in one concentrated attack, when Exeter was targeted not for its limited military or industrial value, but for its cultural worth.

Infuriated by the RAF's destruction of Lübeck, an historic German Baltic city largely built of timber, targeted for supplying the Russian front, Hitler compiled from the Baedeker guide a list of England's civic 'jewels' for destruction. Unhappily, Exeter was the first target, a compliment from the Führer it could have done without. Preliminary raids claimed over a hundred casualties.

After attacking Bath, Norwich, York and Canterbury, the Luftwaffe again easily located Exeter on the moonlit night of 4 May, 1942.

Forty German aircraft flew up the Exe Estuary, dropping 160 high explosive bombs and 10,000 incendiaries on central Exeter in just over one hour – a total payload of seventy-five tonnes. This killed 156 people and injured over 500 more. The devastation over 15 hectares was spectacular. Half the High Street and large areas around South Street, Paris Street and Sidwell Street were either destroyed immediately or in the ensuing conflagration.

Important buildings, including Bampfylde House, the hall of the Vicars Choral, the Abbot's Lodge in the Close, St Luke's College and the city library were badly damaged or destroyed, along with the Lower Market and much of the old City Hospital in Heavitree Road. Six churches were either destroyed or severely damaged, including the medieval church of St Lawrence. The Cathedral was badly mauled.

St Sidwell's, as rebuilt in 1812 and severely damaged by bombing. St Sidwell, or Sativola, was supposedly a local martyr in late Roman or post-Roman times, and the first church was built in the Roman cemetery

Three quarters of the principal shopping area was destroyed, plus a large number of shops, offices and warehouses. Exeter lost 400 of its 1400 shops and 1500 houses out of a stock of 18,500. In addition, 2700 houses were seriously damaged and many more slightly damaged.

When American troops arrived in 1943, Exeter saw racial segregation for the first and only time in its history. Black servicemen stayed in St Thomas, white Americans east of the Exe. Meanwhile, the Exe estuary became a vast military camp in the build-up to D-Day, 1944. The bridges at Countess Wear were used as a practice area for the successful Pegasus Bridge raid in Normandy.

When the war was over, the question of how to rebuild Exeter was addressed by a professional town planner, Thomas Sharp, who published his radical proposals in a book, *Exeter Phoenix*, in 1946. Only part of his plan was realised by the city council, which baulked at the overall cost.

Sharp wanted to keep Exeter's pre-war 'intimacy of scale'. As he proposed, the ruins of St Catherine's almshouses and the Vicar's Choral were kept as war memorials. However, he did not approve of building replicas of damaged or destroyed houses. In his view, the destruction had cleared the way for modernisation. Thus Bedford Circus, badly damaged by the bombing but still standing, was demolished and replaced by Princesshay – yet Princesshay was demolished in its turn in 2005, redeveloped as a shopping and residential centre at a cost of £230 million, and reopened with suitable media fanfare in 2007.

'Strangulation from traffic' was a danger Sharp correctly prophesied. He recommended an inner ring road and a relief for Pinhoe and Blackboy Road. Western Way duly followed in the 1960s, elbowing aside medieval Frog Street.

Also threatened with destruction during the Western Way development was a medieval timber framed house in Edmund Street. This became the focus of international news coverage as 'The House that Moved' when it was jacked up and moved on rollers to its present position in West Street, opposite St Mary Steps, in 1961.

More roads brought more traffic. Devon's leading historian W G Hoskins (who never owned a car and who led the campaign to save The House that Moved) averred: 'People are more important than roads and houses more important than cars'. However, the traffic problem would not go away.

Exeter's outer bypass became notorious for its summer logjams of holidaymakers. And so the M5 was built, reaching Exeter in 1976 and extended over the Exe in 1977. The A38 was upgraded to the 'Devon Expressway'. Yet even these broad highways become clogged with traffic in the twenty-first century.

Another recurrent problem raised its head in 1960. Exeter is partly built on the flood plain of the Exe and has always been liable to inundation. The last hundred years have seen several minor floods and, after the harsh winter of 1917-18 when the Exe froze solid, the resulting meltwater caused severe flooding. However, the heavy autumn rains of 1960 caused worse problems still.

During October 1960, the city was pelted with 380mm of rain – half the *annual* average. The river rose alarmingly on 26 October, when 60mm more rain fell. The next day, 700 cubic metres of water per second barrelled down the Exe from flooded Exmoor and Mid Devon, inundating St Thomas and Exwick to a depth of up to two metres (over six feet) and damaging a thousand shops and homes.

Unless Exeter was defended from the Exe, another such catastrophe seemed inevitable. Between 1965 and 1977 an £8 million (at 1977 prices) flood defence scheme was built. So far, this has been successful.

The scheme covers the river from Cowley Bridge to Countess Wear. It includes three flood relief channels; the most sophisticated, the Exwick Spillway, being controlled by an automatic gate. Integral to it was the replacement of the 1905 Exe Bridge and its narrow channel with the higher twin bridges. These span a smoothed and deepened concrete-lined river channel for faster flow.

Exeter saw other notable developments in the late twentieth century and the start of the twenty-first. Although the city lost the Theatre Royal in 1962, it gained the Northcott Theatre in 1967 and the Phoenix Arts Centre in 1983. Exeter regained its library in 1965, a belated replacement for the one lost in the Blitz.

Exeter University, incorporating St Luke's (Teacher Training) College in 1978, has expanded greatly. Indeed, Exeter is a diverse centre for education. In addition to its respected schools, including Exeter School (1633), Hele's Grammar School (1845) and Maynard School (1876), it has several specialised institutions. These include the Royal School for the Deaf (which began as the Deaf and Dumb Institution, 1826); the West of England School which, under various titles, has taught blind and partially sighted children for 170 years, and St Loye's, a training centre for people with various disabilities, which includes a school of occupational therapy. Exeter's latest contribution to education is the Peninsula Medical School, established in 2000.

Five of Exeter's central churches have been linked in the Central Parish – Saints Stephen, Olave, Pancras, Mary Arches and Petrock's. St Petrock's has been converted into a centre where homeless people (of whom affluent Britain is producing increasing numbers) can get advice, a hot bath and a meal. St Sidwell's has become a community centre.

Industrial estates were part of Thomas Sharp's plan in *Exeter Phoenix*. Marsh Barton has burgeoned and Sowton grown apace beside the M5. A number of banks, insurance companies and hi-tech concerns have relocated to Exeter, the highest profile in recent years being the Meteorological Office in 2003. Perhaps, like so many modern phenomena, this is in imitation of the United States and the widespread move to the Sunshine Belt – though whether Devon qualifies as a British Sunshine Belt is a question best left to the Meteorological Office.

Exeter's long history and – despite the destruction wrought by the Luftwaffe and modern roads – its wonderful heritage of ancient buildings, make it an exceptionally interesting city of great character. Set in a beautiful landscape, it remains one of England's most rewarding cities to study and explore.

A short bibliography

Folkes, John and Margaret, *Exeter Postcards*, Tempus, Stroud, 2005

Gray, Todd, *The Essence of Exeter*, Mint Press, Exeter, 2004

Harvey, Hazel, *Exeter Past*, Phillimore, Chichester, 1996

Hoskins, WG, *Two Thousand Years in Exeter*, Phillimore, Chichester, 1960, 1963 and 2004

Hoskins, WG, *Devon and its People*, David and Charles, Newton Abbot, 1959 and 1968

Lethbridge, Tony, *Exeter: History and Guide*, Tempus, Stroud, 2005

Ordnance Survey map of Exeter and Sidmouth, first produced 1809, reprinted by Cassini (Timeline), 2005

Stoyle, Mark, *Circled with Stone: Exeter's City Walls*, University of Exeter Press, 2003

Stoyle, Mark, *From Deliverance to Destruction: Rebellion and Civil War in an English City*, University of Exeter Press, 1996

Sturt, John, *Revolt in the West: The Western Rebellion of 1549*, Devon Books, Tiverton, 1987

Thomas, Peter, *The Changing Face of Exeter*, Alan Sutton, Stroud, 1995